LET'S GO TO AN
INDIAN CLIFF DWELLING

Hundreds of years ago, Indians living in the southwest part of the United States built apartment houses inside the huge caves on the sides of cliffs. When you visit Mesa Verde National Park, you can examine the ruins of these Indian cliff dwellings and the Indians' places of worship. You can see museum exhibits showing how all groups of Mesa Verde Indians, even those who lived two thousand years ago, ate and slept, hunted and worshipped.

LET'S GO TO AN INDIAN CLIFF DWELLING

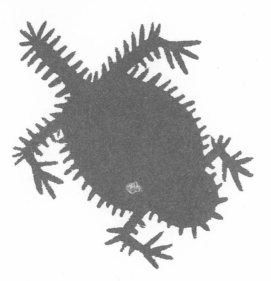

by

BARBARA WILLIAMS

illustrated by

ROBIN KING

G. P. PUTNAM'S SONS   NEW YORK

The author and artist wish to acknowledge the help of Mrs. Jean Pinkley, Chief Archaeologist at Mesa Verde National Park, for her cooperation in the preparation of this book.

571
Wi

How would you like to live in a home built partly underground, a home that had only one door and no windows?

Or how would you like to live in a dark, one-room house built inside a cave on the side of a cliff? Would it frighten you to look out on a "front yard" that fell straight down a 1,000-foot canyon? Would you want to go out to play if it meant that you had to climb up and down dangerous footholds chipped out of rock?

Many hundreds of years ago Indian boys and girls lived in strange houses like these throughout the southwest part of the United States. Today you may visit ruins of some of these homes on a great, flat-topped hill in Colorado called the Mesa Verde (MAY-sah VER-day) or "green tableland."

Arriving at Mesa Verde National Park, you go first to the museum at Park Headquarters. Here a ranger gives you a booklet showing a map of the park and explains the guided tours you may take. But he urges you first to study the exhibits in the museum itself.

You walk down a narrow hall, and to your left are five dioramas, scenes made with doll-like figures, showing how the Mesa Verde Indians lived. Little signs help you to understand each scene.

As you pass by the dioramas and examine each one, you see the five periods in the development of the ancient Indians who lived at or near Mesa Verde.

More than ten thousand years ago, bands of Indians who hunted wild animals roamed near Mesa Verde. They slept out in the open, using only trees for shelter. Because their food was the game which they killed and ate, they kept moving around, following the animals.

The first group of Indians to live at Mesa Verde came about the time that Christ was born. They found shelter in the great natural caves in the canyons and raised corn and squash on the mesa top. For hunting they used a weapon called an atlatl (at-LAT-ul), a throwing-stick which hurls long darts. These Indians made baskets of many shapes and designs and are called Basket Makers.

The Modified Basket Makers were the next group of Mesa Verde Indians. Built partly underground, their pit houses looked like square hills of adobe (a-DOH-be) clay. These Indians started making pottery, which could be put directly over a fire and which added many new kinds of cooked foods to their diet.

Little by little the Indians changed their houses. They started building homes that joined together in long, curving rows. Today we call these dwellings pueblos (PWEB-lohs), which is the Spanish word for "villages." The Indians who lived in them are known as the Developmental Pueblos.

The last group of Indians, who lived at Mesa Verde during the Great Pueblo Period, built fine villages inside caves. Some pueblos had hundreds of rooms and looked like our modern apartment houses. But for some reason the Mesa Verde Indians left their homes about two hundred years before white men came to America. The once-proud cities were left to crumble away into dust.

How do people today know what these different groups of Mesa Verde Indians ate and how they lived? Archaeologists, the men who study what was left by people who died long ago, have found pottery, baskets, weapons, and many other things belonging to these ancient Indians. You will see how archaeologists have put together the Mesa Verde story when you visit the museum exhibits. You turn right and walk down some stairs.

In the first room, you are startled to walk right up to two mummies. One is of a woman about twenty years old, the other is of a small boy. These mummies were discovered with seventeen others in a cave where the dry air saved them. They are Indians of the Basket Maker Period, the people who lived about 2,000 years ago. The woman mummy has her hair hacked off, but on the wall are pictures of some men's long, fancy hair styles. Later, in the museum, when you see ropes made of human hair, you will wonder how the woman felt when she had her hair cut.

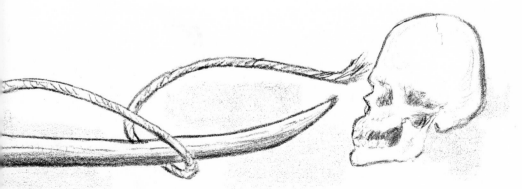

You notice other interesting exhibits. You see the "medicines" in a witch doctor's "little black bag" and wonder how he used them. There are colored stones, cords, and even more strange, a small piece of leather wrapped around a sawed-off human thumb. You notice also the beautiful baskets, the turkey-feather blankets, the sandals, and the many pieces of pottery.

Skulls in another room show the crooked and diseased teeth which must have given many Mesa Verde Indians bad toothaches. Even the adults lucky enough to have healthy teeth wore them away a little nearly every time they ate. Some wore their teeth almost to the gum line from the sandstone powder in their food. The Indians ground their corn on sandstone metates (meh-TAH-tays), and bits of rock broke off into the meal.

Leaving the museum, you are eager to see the real Indian ruins. You turn left and walk a few steps to Spruce Tree House path. Along the path you notice the twisted junipers. You keep away from the prickly yucca plants, but you see the thin threads running through their long, sharp leaves. The Indians used yucca fiber to weave most of their baskets and sandals. You also see the tall Douglas firs which the men who discovered Spruce Tree House called spruces. An artist with a set of water colors is sitting on a rock painting, and you stop to view the scene as he sees it.

There is a huge cave formed in the sandstone cliff by water oozing in a little at a time. In this cave is a village just like the one you saw in the last museum diorama. True, some of the walls have broken into small pieces and fallen, and the people walking about are white men in modern clothes. But you can imagine that you have traveled back seven hundred years in time, and Indians are going about their work in Spruce Tree House. You hurry down the path for a closer look.

Spruce Tree House once held 114 sleeping rooms and eight rooms for worship, called kivas (KEE-vahs). Each room was a separate house, belonging to the wife of the family. She built her house either next to her mother's house or on top of it. The houses were very small, about six by eight feet square and five and one-half feet high. They were also dark, stuffy, and cold in winter. Probably the people used them only for sleeping. Sometimes the men spent the night in the more comfortable kivas.

You step into the courtyard and look down into a kiva, the roof of which has broken into tiny pieces and disappeared. Most kivas are round, underground rooms about twelve feet across and eight feet deep. The walls are lined with stone to hold them up better. Each kiva has a ledge running around the room, a round fire pit in the floor, and a narrow space for air. Most kivas also have a smaller round hole in the floor known as a sipapu (SEE-PAH-POOH). The Indians believed that their spirits came to this world from the center of the earth through a hole called the Sipapu. But the hole in the kiva floor is merely an imitation or a symbol of the real Sipapu.

Three kivas at Spruce Tree House have been completely rebuilt, and you enter one by going through a hole in the roof and climbing down a ladder. In this room, hundreds of years ago, the men taught the boys the important dances and songs that they must use to please the sun and rain gods. Here also the men played games and taught the boys to weave cotton fabrics and to make the warm turkey-feather blankets that everyone needed in winter. Even modern Pueblo Indians allow women in the kivas only at special times. Very likely this custom began hundreds of years ago.

Up above in the courtyard, the young girls once gathered to watch their mothers grind corn and nuts in the grinding bin. The women knelt with their heels against the wall to be better balanced as they rubbed the small hand-stone, or mano (MAH-no), against the large flat metate. It was important for the girls to watch their mothers, for unless they learned to grind corn well, they would never be chosen as wives. Their mothers also showed them how to make yucca-leaf brooms and tiny pottery dishes for their dolls.

The girls helped their mothers by tending the smaller children. Tiny babies were strapped to hard wooden cradle boards. This helped prevent falls in the steep canyons. But the cradle boards flattened the backs of the babies' heads, and the Indians of the later Mesa Verde periods grew up with flat skulls.

When the older girls and boys didn't have jobs to do, they could play with each other or with their pets. Some of the children kept dogs, as you do, but other children had turkeys for pets.

It is hard to believe that the Indians who built these round kivas and straight-edged houses had no compasses, no rulers, no tools of any kind except crude stones. Spruce Tree House was built by the last group of Mesa Verde Indians. During this Great Pueblo Period the finest homes were put up.

Although the pit houses on the mesa top were not as well made as the cliff dwellings of the Great Pueblo Period, in one way they are more important. By studying the pit house ruins, archaeologists have learned how the Indian homes developed over the years. Part of each pit house was built underground. When you visit the pit house ruins in the order they were built, you see that the earliest ones were made over shallow pits. Bit by bit, after several hundred years, the pits became deeper until the Indians built kivas (for worshipping their gods) completely underground. Their homes were then built aboveground, usually next to each other, in villages. Near the pit house ruins you see where such a village, Sun Point Pueblo, once stood.

Like their Basket Maker ancestors, the Modified Basket Makers who lived in the pit houses hunted game for most of their food. But they used the bow and arrow, which was a better weapon than the atlatl of the earlier Indians. With a bow and arrow they could take careful aim. They could also hide in the bushes where the animals could not see them. The boys were very proud when they could shoot a squirrel, a rabbit, or even a mountain sheep for their mothers to cook.

Both the Basket Makers and Modified Basket Makers had long skulls. They kept their babies on soft, padded cradles which permitted the babies' heads to grow in a normal way.

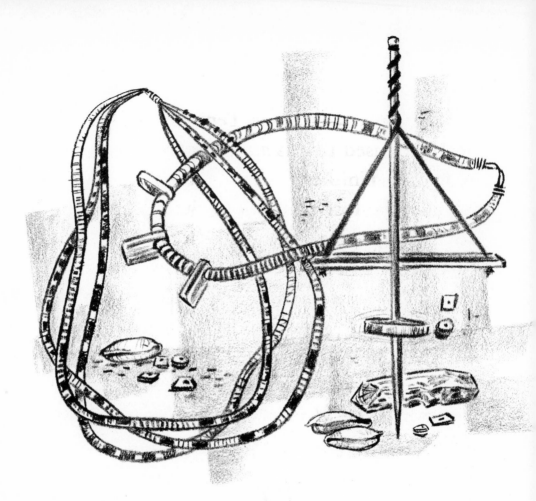

Although they wore few clothes, these early people wore necklaces and other jewelry made from stones, shells, bones, and seeds. They may have traded corn or baskets with other Indians living to the west for the rare sea shells.

The next stop is at Sun Temple. The Indians probably used this as a place of worship, not as a home. Unlike the other Mesa Verde ruins, which have lost their roofs, Sun Temple has no roof because it was never finished. You climb about eleven feet up a ladder and stand on one of the walls for a view. Sun Temple is shaped like a huge letter D formed by two thick walls on every side. The narrow space between the two walls is separated into small rooms in which the Indians may have planned their festivals or stored their food and baskets.

You drive past a field where archaeologists
are growing corn by the old methods the Indians used. At a spot near Cliff Palace, you
wait for the ranger who will take you on your
first guided tour. In the distance you can see
the people on another tour just ahead of yours.

From this lookout point the cave itself is
easily seen. Cliff Palace cave is 350 feet long
and 100 feet deep. It is set into steep rock, with
a canyon below. The Indian men, carrying
their game or crops, once lowered themselves
from the mesa top by dangerous toe and hand

holds cut in the sandstone. The women had to climb up the rough sides of the canyon from the spring below balancing five-gallon jugs of water on their heads. But the Indians moved to this hard-to-reach cave from their homes on the flat mesa top because here it would be easier to fight off their enemies.

Some of the Cliff Palace homes have doors and windows, but others were probably entered through the roofs. The rooms without windows were very likely used to store food.

33

You notice the round tower of Cliff Palace, which is one of the most interesting buildings in Mesa Verde.

Your guide tells you that Cliff Palace, the largest Mesa Verde cliff dwelling, was discovered by white men in 1888. At that time it had not been lived in for six hundred years. The white men had heard from their Indian friends about a huge dwelling on the side of a cliff. But the Indians were afraid to go near it. They thought that evil spirits might live in it.

As you come close to Cliff Palace, you can see that some of it is built high up, some very low. In some places, it reaches up to four stories high. Not all of the rooms contain fireplaces. The Indians probably found that it was better to be cold than to breathe in the smoke from a fire in a closed room.

Your guide points out how carefully the buildings were put up. He shows how evenly the stones were cut and laid. Many of the rooms are decorated, but the third-floor room of the great four-story tower is the most beautiful home in Mesa Verde. All four walls are painted in pretty red and white designs.

Leaving Cliff Palace, you head for the spot where you will meet your guide for your spooky trip to Balcony House. Although an easy path has been built part of the way to the ruin, Balcony House is still hard to reach. Your guide tells you to lock away your purses and cameras in your car so that your hands will be free. You will have to crawl through a dark tunnel and climb several ladders.

The tour begins down a small hill. But you soon come to a long flight of steep steps leading down, down, down. You can imagine how difficult the route must have been before the steps were built. The guide points out the thirty-foot double ladder you must climb up. He gives visitors careful rules for their safety.

The ladder sways under the load of all the people climbing on it. This frightens you a little, and you do not look below to the steep canyon. The guide takes your hand to pull you up the last step, and you reach the most exciting location of all the Mesa Verde ruins: Balcony House. The second-story balcony, or porch, built for added working space because there was no room in front of the dwelling, looks almost the way it did hundreds of years ago. The wall in front of the ruin is as carefully curved against the weight of the earth as a dam is arched by the most modern engineers.

Now you get down on your hands and knees

to crawl through a dark tunnel. Two more short ladders bring you once more to the mesa top.

You want to take one final look at the park. Going past the Indians' farms, on many levels, you see Cedar Tree Tower. Once probably the place where the Indians noisily worshipped the gods, Cedar Tree Tower stands empty and quiet. Why did the Indians leave the Mesa Verde? Were they driven out by enemies who came sweeping down from the north? Did they fight among themselves? Did they leave in search of food after the terrible dry spell that lasted for twenty-three years?

Archaeologists do not know for sure.

But you leave Mesa Verde, wondering what became of the long-ago people who built the strange and interesting homes on the top, in the caves, and even under the earth of the "green tableland."

GLOSSARY

ADOBE — a kind of clay that gets very hard when it is dried in the sun.

ARCHAEOLOGIST — a scientist who studies objects and bones left by people who died long ago.

ATLATL — a throwing-stick once used to hurl long darts.

BASKET MAKER PERIOD — the period of time between the birth of Christ and 450 A.D. when the Mesa Verde Indians learned to make baskets.

DEVELOPMENTAL PUEBLO PERIOD — the period of time between 750 A.D. and 1100 A.D. when the Mesa Verde Indians developed their ability to make pottery and houses.

DIORAMA — a scene made with doll-like figures.

EXHIBIT — an object or group of objects being shown in a museum.

FIBER — a tough material composed of threadlike parts.

GAME — animals hunted for food.

GREAT PUEBLO PERIOD — the period of time between 1100 A.D. and 1300 A.D. when the Mesa Verde Indians made their finest homes and pottery.

KIVA — a round underground room used for religious ceremonies and as a clubhouse for the men.

MANO — the small handstone used to grind corn.

MEAL — a coarsely ground grain.

MESA VERDE — a large, flat-topped hill in southwestern Colorado, covered with evergreen trees. Name means "green tableland" in Spanish.

METATE — a large flat stone on which the smaller mano is rubbed to grind corn.

MODIFIED BASKET MAKER PERIOD — the period of time between 450 A.D. and 750 A.D. when the Mesa Verde Indians learned to make crude pottery as well as beautiful baskets. The people lived in pit houses and started raising beans.

MUMMY — the dried-up (and well-preserved) body of a dead person.

PIT HOUSE — a house made of poles and adobe plaster over a pit in the ground.

PUEBLO — Spanish word for "village." Indians of any tribe who build their homes touching each other are called Pueblo Indians.

RUIN — the fallen or crumbling remains of an old house or city.

SANDSTONE — a kind of rock which breaks up into sand.

SIPAPU — the hole which the Pueblo Indians believe they used to enter this world from the center of the earth. Most kiva floors have small holes which are symbols of the real Sipapu.

SKULL — the bony part of a head.

SPRING — a small stream of water.

SYMBOL — something that stands for something else.

Other Things to Do While Reading
Let's Go to an Indian Cliff Dwelling

1. Using one of the author's explanations of what might have happened to the Cliff Dwellers, write a short story. Tell in detail where they went and why. You might want to include a guess about where their ancestors are today.
2. Try making your own pottery with clay.
3. Draw a scene showing how the Cliff Dwellers did some of the things we do today (eat, cook, get food, sleep, etc.).
4. Who first discovered the cliff dwellings? How long ago?
5. If you are a girl, pretend to be a girl Cliff Dweller. Write about the chores you do to help your mother. If you are a boy, pretend to be a boy Cliff Dweller. Write a paragraph describing the ways in which you help your father.
6. Make a short picture dictionary of the words which you are meeting for the first time. Print each word in large letters. Then print a short definition of the word. Draw a picture to illustrate the word.
7. Try balancing a book on your head as you climb the stairs. You will get some idea of how the Cliff Dwellers carried water up to their homes.

Other Books about Cliff Dwellers

1. Fenton, Carroll L., and Epstein, Alice, *Cliff Dwellers of Walnut Canyon.* John Day.
2. Floethe, Louise, *Indian and His Pueblo.* Scribner.
3. James, Harry C., *Day in Oraibi, a Hopi Indian Village.* Melmont.

OTHER TITLES IN THE POPULAR *LET'S GO* SERIES

Science

for a Nature Walk
to a Planetarium
to a Rocket Base
on a Space Trip
to a Weather Station
to the Moon

Health

to a Dentist
to a Hospital

Communications

to a Telephone Company
to a Television Station

Food and Clothing

to a Bakery
to a Candy Factory
to a Clothing Factory
to a Dairy
to a Farm

Commerce and Industry

to an Automobile Factory
Logging
to an Oil Refinery
to a Steel Mill

Transportation

to an Airport
to a Freight Yard
to a Harbor
to a Truck Terminal

Conservation

to a Dam
to a National Park

American History

to Colonial Williamsburg
to Mount Vernon
to an Indian Cliff Dwelling

Armed Services

to Annapolis
to the U.S. Air Force Academy
to West Point
to the U.S. Coast Guard Academy
aboard an Atomic Submarine

Government — Local

to a City Hall
to a Court
to Vote

Government — National and International

to the Capitol
to the F.B.I.
to the Supreme Court
to the United Nations Headquarters
to the U.S. Mint
to the White House

Recreation

to an Aquarium
to a Circus
to a World's Fair
to a Zoo

Music and Art

to an Art Museum
to a Ballet
to a Concert

Community — Commercial

to a Bank
to a Garage
to a Newspaper
to a Supermarket
to Watch a Building Go Up

Community — Government

to a Firehouse
to a Library
to a Police Station
to a Post Office
to a Sanitation Department
to a School